Letting go of Fear
Walking in Freedom

LETTING GO OF *FEAR,* WALKING IN FREEDOM

DOREEN GRADY

Copyright © 2019 by Doreen Grady

Letting go of Fear, Walking in Freedom

Printed in the United States of America

First Printing, 2019

ISBN:9781797426891

Cover Designer:
Christopher Davis, Jr. for Ascension Marketing

This book is dedicated to GiGi's heart, my smart, handsome, and amazing grandson, Aari.

You are my inspiration because you have been fighting since day one and have surpassed every challenge presented to you. My desire for you is to dream big and shoot for the galaxy with everything you want to accomplish. Never let anyone talk against the dreams inside of you.

Know that you are never too old to go for what you want, Gigi didn't. Love you to life.

Acknowledgments

I would like to personally thank the following individuals for their words of encouragement, prayers, feedback, critiques, support and above all their love. When I did not think that this would ever come to fruition, you all continued to push me until I found the courage to turn what seemed to be an impossibility into a possibility. For that, I say thank you.

A special thank you to my children, Stephanie and Corey who always believed in me and never let up. Also, to the matriarch of our family, affectionately known to everyone as, "Granny." I thank you for keeping me sharp. I would like to thank my God-daughters Trashell and Kristian, who offered their time, talents and support from the beginning. You loved me through the craziness and for that I say thank you.

Also, I want to thank the Ink Pen Diva herself, Tamika Sims, she pushed until I birthed this baby. She never sugar coated the truth, but made me push through the pain.

Finally, I would like to thank the one who makes ALL things possible. He is the Author and the Finisher of my faith. He is my Heavenly Father. He is the only man who has never left me. God, I thank You for consistently showing me who You truly are in my life. A favorite scripture of mine that has always kept me grounded is Jeremiah 29:11 which reads, *"For I know the thoughts that I think toward you, saith the Lord, thoughts of peace, and not of evil, to give you an expected end."*

God, I thank you for my expected end.

CONTENTS

FOREWORD

I have the distinct honor of writing this for an outstanding young woman who has beaten great odds and overcome many obstacles in her life. It was clearly the grace of God that brought her through. This young woman kept on fighting so that other women who share the same struggles, can experience the same victory she has. I believe that her life experience will both touch and inspire many to keep fighting and never give up on themselves. I believe that every one of us has a book on the inside of us. Therefore, I encourage everyone to both read and share this story with a family member or a friend.

Galatians 6:7 reminds us that, *"Whatsoever a man soweth, that shall he also reap."*

If this is true, your reading and sharing of her story may be the seed that brings forth the fruit of someone reading and sharing yours.

—Bishop Spencer H. Riddick, Jr.

Founder of New Abundant Life Christian Center Portsmouth, VA

INTRODUCTION

Dear Readers,

I wanted to share my story and my heart. As hard as it was to relive my past it was necessary because everything I've gone through has made me into the person I am today. I have no regrets because it was a process to get me to my purpose. If you are currently in the thick of it all, know it is for a reason and only a specific time period.

The process reveals how much we are capable of handling whether we believe it or not. There were times I didn't believe I could take any more, but I would wake up the next day to do it all over again. During this process, hold your head up high, stay focused, and keep moving until you are on the other side of the pain. It is true, trouble don't last always.

Also, the process is not a place to remain, but to go through. According to *Merriam Webster,*process is defined as: *a natural phenomenon marked by gradual changes that lead toward a particular result; the process of growth.* Process is not permanent and don't allow it to become your normal but push through to get all that you have been destined to receive.

"In you, LORD my God, I put my trust."

—Psalm 25:1

CHAPTER ONE

The Onset

To be deceived a lie must be established early to be effective. In the Garden of Eden, the enemy told Eve, "you won't surely die," if you eat the fruit, (Genesis 3:4). That was Eve's buy-in to the lie. A lie is a false statement deliberately presented as being true, a falsehood. Something meant to deceive or give a wrong impression; to present false information with the intention of deceiving. This is how the enemy uses lies to present his plan to deceive us. Also, lies presented early in life are most effective.

I grew up in a home with both parents working. Daycare was not an option. I lived with my grandparents the first five years of my life. My father did not keep steady employment. My mom carried the load of the household consistently being the primary breadwinner. Mom was a teacher and back in the 60's, teachers did not get paid during the summer, but she made sure I didn't lack for anything.

I was told my father had good jobs, but he had two downfalls, women and drinking. The enemy set in motion early in my life that I never saw any real men. My father drank heavily and never lived up to his responsibilities as a husband and father. I loved my father, he had good intentions, but consistently failed the task. What I was being exposed to set the example/standard for me with relationships. The short period my dad was in the home he provided no guidance or real interaction.

A deadly combination was formed, low/no self-esteem + no positive male influence = disaster. Fathers help give their daughters their identity; without that, we struggle to find who we are. I grew up as a very shy overweight girl who just wanted to fit in, but never did.

The nickname given to me by my uncle was not flattering or cute to say the least. My nick name was "tooty pounder;" short for 200 pounder. This did wonders for my self-esteem. Pun intended. I didn't have any. I began to see myself differently from everyone else. Some members of my family thought it was funny for me to be called by this name. My grandmother who was called, "Big Momma" was always my hiding place when I got sad from being teased. The source of my strength back then and my solace was having her give me food.

This further caused me pain because I was teased for always eating. It wasn't so much what Big Momma said, but how she made me feel. She made me feel loved and safe no matter what. She never spoke a negative word towards me. My Big Momma only displayed strength and grace. This grace was needed when my grandfather passed.

My can-daddy, (as I called him), and I shared a special bond. He was my playmate. After he passed, I would still see him sitting in his favorite spot on the front porch. When Big Momma and I would go to bed, I could feel my can-daddy tickling my feet. I would be giggling and laughing and telling him to stop. Big Momma never seemed to think this was strange and would just say, "Walter, leave her alone and let her sleep." When I shared this with other family members they would ask why I wasn't scared to see my granddaddy?

This was not strange to me because this is what we always did together. I did not understand him being dead or not being there because to me he still was. When I asked Big Momma how I could see him, and should I be afraid? Her response was your grandfather has always loved you and would never hurt you, but the moment you become afraid you won't see him anymore.

Others opinions and fears overshadowed our fun and made me feel different and odd. Fear took over and I never saw my can-daddy again. Bitterness was established at that moment between me and members of my family. I never realized that the effects of my childhood would shape or play a vital part of who I would become as an adult.

This became my period of discovery, and I kept asking the question, "Who am I?" For years, I did not know the answer because I was preoccupied with the constant situations and problems that plagued my life. "Why do I seem to not fit in anywhere?" "Why do I feel less than?" Not realizing at the time the battlefield was my mind and the enemy, (or inner me), was using my past to try to hinder my future. The sad part is I allowed this mindset. I had not realized at the time, the questions I was asking God had already been answered in His Word. I had to learn to see myself as God sees me despite my current situation.

This period forced me to face some hard truths. I was never designed to, "fit in." I have always been a thumb. Look at the design of your hand. The thumb is off to itself, still attached, but has its own identity independent of the other fingers. To create my own independence, I came up with an acronym for **t.h.u.m.b.**; totally humble and uniquely mind blowing. I know it may be a little cheesy, but I came up with ways to fit that spoke life to me.

Dancing was also part of my self-discovery. No organized classes just putting on some upbeat music and just moving. This was loads of fun. In my Bible Study time God's Word was constantly reminding me that I am the head and not the tail; above and not beneath.

I was wanting and seeking affirmation from others and had to go back and find the root of these feelings. What

I realized was that I had blocked out a very damaging part of my past and needed to deal with the hurt and devastated little girl that I hadn't given a voice too.

"Thou wilt keep him in perfect peace, whose mind is stayed on thee: because he trusteth in thee."

—Isaiah 26:3

CHAPTER TWO

Hush ... You Don't Matter

I remember I was around six years old, scared, angry, and hurt because I didn't believe some members of my family loved me, only tolerated me. Those members of my family included my aunt, uncle, and cousin; who I would come to find out was my sister. We will talk about that a little later.

When I visited my aunt and uncle there were some good times. My cousin and I would pick grapes from the vine in the backyard or watch the big gold fish in the pond. Then there were the other times I would be talked about because I was chubby and loved to talk. I would be talking to my cousin and she would get up and put on this record, "You talk too much," and laugh. I would immediately shut down and she got what she wanted... me quiet. That started a divide between us that grew as we got older. I wanted so much to please them, but nothing was ever good enough.

My mom and dad also separated for the first time when I was six. I would hear my aunt talking about my daddy to my mom telling her how he was no good and she should never go back to him. One Saturday, my daddy was coming to see me at my Big Momma's house. I am not sure if someone told me he was coming, or if I saw him coming down the sidewalk, but I started running towards the storm door to get to him. When I reached the door, the latch didn't open because it was locked. I was running so fast I couldn't stop, and I went through the glass.

Glass was all over me, but the only injury was a cut to my elbow. A miracle. I was screaming and crying, and all my aunt said was, "You shouldn't have been running." That statement hurt me and again, I shut down. My Big Momma gathered me up and told me I would be ok and that I didn't have to go to the hospital for stitches. She told me she would take care of me and she did. I carry that scar on my elbow to this day.

Little Doreen was also hiding a dark secret that had happened during this same time frame between ages five and six.

It was during a conversation with my daughter when we were talking about women who were coming forth to say they had been molested 10-15 years prior. She asked why come forward now after so many years? In trying to answer that question for those women, my past came flooding back. It was then that I realized I had been molested as a child. It happened over 50 years ago and the person responsible was the older female cousin of one of my friends. She would make me, and my friends, lie on the ground and touch us inappropriately below the waist. We never talked about the experience or told anyone out of fear and embarrassment.

We tend to bury/hide things from our past because we are trying to forget. Sharing my experience with my daughter, allowed me to feel free and I imagined those women were now coming forward because they were ready to confront their issue. So now was my time to confront my issue. After coming to terms with this revelation, I told my mom.

When I shared this experience with her, we both cried. I cried as a freeing and my mom cried because she was hurt that she didn't protect me. She also stated it was for the best I hadn't told her sooner because she would probably just be getting out of jail had she known back then.

During my adolescent years and while in junior high school, my aunt had me over her house one day. While there, she said there was something I needed to know, and she told me my cousin, (her daughter), was really my sister. I was shocked and in disbelief. I told her I didn't believe her and her response was, "Believe what you want, it is the truth, end of story." She provided no further information. Once I got home, my momma provided all the missing pieces. This was still difficult to process, but I had to accept the truth. I wanted to know why my Aunt felt the need to tell me something that my Mom should have told me. Again, I felt as if I didn't matter and another reason to shut down.

My journey must show the history behind some of the choices in my life and reveal the cause so freedom can take place.

"If you don't transform from your pain it was for nothing."
— **Author Unknown**

"But ye are a chosen generation, a royal priesthood, an holy nation, a peculiar people; that ye should shew forth the praises of him who hath called you out of darkness into his marvellous light: "

—1 Peter 2:9

CHAPTER THREE

Science & Invisibility Continues

High school was uneventful for me, except for my two best friends. We practically did everything together. Sleepovers were a major part of our weekends. They were my life in high school. Friday night football games were the best because we were all in the band together. Outside of band there was nothing for me. I didn't date. I watched my friends date and have boyfriends, but I remained on the sidelines, invisible.

This invisibility hindered me throughout my three years of high school. I wasn't comfortable in my own skin, so I didn't allow anyone outside of my circle to see me. I didn't walk around sad and unhappy. Nobody ever knew how I felt about feeling invisible. I learned from my childhood how to mask my feelings and keep everything inside.

When I did show interest in a boy after prompting from my friends, it wasn't reciprocated. One guy told me I was too fat, and he wasn't interested. The irony is I was not fat, but to a 15, 16-year-old boy, I seemed huge. Looking back, I would love to be that size again.

A highlight was getting my license at 16. My friends and I would take turns driving to our favorite spot, Giant Open-Air Market on the weekends. We would order pizza, laugh and talk for hours, or at least until our curfew. The memory that stands out the most for me from high school was planning and decorating my senior prom.

I remember the theme of the prom was, "Stairway to Heaven," by the O'Jays. We put a lot of time and energy to making the facility beautiful, only for me to go home because no one had asked me to go. I don't think I even cried that night because this was something that was familiar to me and I just accepted. These memories let me know it was not my size that wasn't attractive, but my lack of self-confidence and low self-esteem. A self-confident woman is very attractive and naturally radiates beauty.

In preparing for college and meeting with Guidance Counselors, I wasn't given any direction towards a goal or a career objective. All I knew is that I did not want to teach anyone's kids. I ended up settling for a generic curriculum in Business. When I graduated from high school at 17, I was ready to take on the world. Not really, I was not mentally or socially ready to go away to school. Nor was I pushed to leave home.

When I arrived on Norfolk State College, (now University), campus, I was considerably smaller and a little confident. Still somewhat shy, I was glad some friends from high school were there to help with the transition. I didn't stay on campus and commuted every day. There was no financial aid, my mom funded my college tuition.

My best friends went to other schools, but we stayed in touch. It was through my best friend, who remained local, that I met my first boyfriend during my freshman year. He was an upperclassman from Nigeria. Dating was new for me. I had no experience and no one to prepare me for the games. My best friend always tried to school me on dating, but life turned out to be the greatest teacher.

College was the best time of my life. Still the shy little girl, but because people were always around, it was easy to hide in the background and still be a part of the fun. My first heartbreak came when I started gaining weight and my boyfriend wanted to break up. He said I was getting to big for him. I was devastated. The pain I was experiencing was foreign to me.

I could not handle it and I went to stay with a friend to try and get over this heartache. It felt as if I was reliving my childhood again and I would always be that fat unloved little girl.

Still not confident in who I was and struggling with my self-esteem, I was always looking for someone else willing to validate me or prove my worth. The negative comments from past experiences with my family started to resurface. I honestly believed I should be grateful anyone showed me any attention because of how I looked.

Some friends and I decided to pledge a sorority during our junior year to get a sense of belonging. I wanted the sisterhood feeling that we were told about in looking at the different organizations. My mom pledged a sorority while she was in college and she told me you can pledge anything you want, but if you want me to pay for it, it will be a certain one. It was 24 of us online and it was an amazing and crazy ride. I was so glad I got to go home at the end of the day and not be in the dorms. It was such a privilege and honor once we were done, to be named as a member of the oldest black sorority.

Leaving Norfolk State was bittersweet, but not for long because I landed a job at the University and stayed there for several years. My life was beginning.

"A good name is rather to be chosen than great riches, and loving favour rather than silver and gold."

—Proverbs 22:1

CHAPTER FOUR

Love Misdirected

The lack of positive men, or men period in my life growing up, set my path in motion for unhealthy relationships. Only three men were in my young life, my granddaddy, who died when I was six, my father who I have no vivid memories of doing anything for me or with me, and my uncle who teased me.

Fear, intimidation, and low self-esteem had become my identity. These behaviors had been with me since childhood. I would later discover what they were really called and how to end this craziness.

When you identify behaviors that are negatively repeated in you or your family, pray and take authority over them. If this is something you are not familiar with, nor know how to do, let me show you what transpired in my life because I did not know either.

My father did not give me my identity growing up and this caused me to look for love in all the wrong places. Fear of being alone, glad to have someone show me attention and affection, ultimately led to multiple relationships and three failed marriages.

My first marriage lasted three years and I endured three years of mental abuse. At 23, I was young and very naïve. My husband was very jealous and constantly accused me of being unfaithful. I was working at a local university during our marriage and on some days, I was embarrassed to go to work. He would put hickeys all over my neck and sometimes my face to let other men know I was taken. This was very awkward for me dealing with the public, but I put a smile on my face, kept to myself when I could and pushed through.

My husband was in the Navy and when his tour was up, he returned to his home state. He had gone ahead to find us a place to live. I put in my notice at work and went one weekend with my three-month-old baby to view our home. I was completely broke and had to borrow money for my plane ticket because I was too afraid to ask my husband.

On the last day after being there a week, I had to let him know I didn't have any money to purchase my plane ticket home. I noticed he had an uncashed check on the dresser from his current job. I asked for money and his response was to get back home the best way I could.

I had to leave and asked for a ride to the airport. There was no conversation during the car ride. When we arrived at the airport, he stopped. I gathered my things and my baby, and he drove off again. There were no words spoken between us. I was stranded with no money in another state. I called one of my best friends and she charged my plane ticket, so I could get home. I never cried, just held onto my baby, boarded the plane and never looked back.

The results for me at the end of my marriage were bitterness, anger, and hatred of all men. I didn't even want men to speak to me. On top of the existence of fear, intimidation, and low self-esteem, I had now added bitterness, anger, and hatred. These emotions began to display immediately upon returning home because life didn't stop. I had to return to work and embrace my new life as a single mom.

A very good friend who worked with me noticed my behavior and attitude. She let me know I didn't have to behave this way. I had developed a potty mouth and would pop off anytime. I had this coffee mug on my desk that stated, "I don't give a$ # * @ . "

My friend hated that mug. We shared many conversations regarding God's love for me and how He wanted me whole and at peace. I did not understand this peace she spoke about or displayed, but knew I wanted the same thing. She never judged me concerning my behavior or my past, she only loved me and introduced me to a man she knew who could help me, His Name was Jesus.

It would be 10 years before I entered another relationship. I was focused on building my relationship with Christ and became very involved with my new church family.

I met my second husband through my best friend. He was quiet, but he was attentive, loving, and romantic. All the things I craved. After one year of dating, we married.

Then one day my world was turned upside down. My brother-in-law brought a piece of mail to the house and told me I needed to read it. The piece of mail was a legal document showing my husband being sued for back child support totaling $30,000. That was not the alarming fact. The woman suing my husband had, "our," last name. My husband told me he had never been married. All of this happened while my husband was overseas.

I did some research on the woman's name on the document and for $8.00 received a copy of their marriage certificate showing my husband's name and signature. It felt like my heart had been ripped out. Ultimately, this meant my marriage was not legal because my husband never divorced his first wife.

Another marriage ended after four years, and I was still struggling to know my value. I had recently joined a ministry that focused on the, "hurting and bruised." The pastor had shared a dream/vision of all these hurting and broken animals coming into the church and I knew that was where I belonged to get the healing I needed. And begin to know who I was and how important I was to God.

As I was moving in the right direction, old feelings began to resurface and I began wanting to be in a committed relationship. Again, looking for love when I hadn't learned to love myself.

I went on a blind date setup by mutual friends. We met at the mall and talked for a couple of hours. He was a good listener. At the end of our date, he asked for a ride home because his car was in the shop and his brother had dropped him off. Reluctantly, I gave in, (red flag, but ignored), and gave him a ride home. Once we got to his house, he asked me to come inside. I declined, but he insisted he wanted me to meet someone. I go inside and the person he wanted me to meet was his mother! Along with his grandmother who also lived there. They were both very sweet and he told me was their caregiver. This was dear to my heart, as I was my mom's caregiver.

We began dating and the car that was in the shop never materialized. Again, so desperate for male companionship, I settled. I did not seek God concerning this relationship. This man was working a minimal job, no car, and living with his mom. Within a few months, we were married. I told myself I could see his potential. He had a lot of redeeming qualities, or so I thought. The voice of reason, (God), was speaking and I didn't listen. I ended up in a crazy situation asking God, why? God was saying, I tried to talk to you and warn you. Then I turned to God to get me out of the mess. What I could not see was my self-worth.

This man totally changed the atmosphere in my home. He and my son didn't have a good relationship, and this caused tension and arguing, both of which had not been part of our home.

My husband's mom became ill and soon passed away. This was devastating for him and he began to drink. A few months later, his aunt died and then his grandmother, several months later. The three women he loved most, were gone. Understandably, this was more than most people go through in a lifetime and he became very angry. His drinking worsened daily and what I didn't know at the time is that drugs had become part of the picture. All the while, I'm trying to paint this picture that our family was fine and hiding the truth from family, friends and my children.

I had a Ford Focus at that time, our only vehicle. My husband took it one night and never came home. I was panicking and calling his cell phone, but to no avail. When he did arrive home, it was without my car. His story was he had left it somewhere, but was going back to get it.

What I found out, through his brother, is that he had traded my car to drug dealers. My husband checked into rehab and I agreed to stay with him. This was my third marriage and I was embarrassed. My husband purchased a van for me to help get things right. Things were better, but he was still struggling with the deaths. We tried pastoral counseling, but it doesn't work if only one spouse is willing to try. Then things started missing from the home. I knew what was happening and again

CHAPTER FIVE

Forgive Yourself = Renewal

S omeone shared on Facebook, *"You date at the level of your self-esteem."* Those nine words rang so loud in my heart and sums up this book in the beginning. My self-esteem issues, fear, and invisibility resulted in the choices I made. I had to forgive me for the choices I made. I learned from those choices and now give myself permission to move forward and do the things that bring me satisfaction. Those choices also resulted in loss of friendships and betrayal of friends who I thought would be a part of my life 'til the end and with no explanation of why they left.

My revelation and healing process came through feeding my faith with the Word of God. According to Merriam Webster, the definition of revelation is, *an enlightening or astonishing disclosure; something that is revealed by God to humans.* As I grew spiritually and understood what belonged to me and the authority I have, I could no longer remain the same.

If your mind is renewed, then you change your declarations about yourself as well as your situations. Speak life to your dead situations. One of my favorite scriptures is:

Jeremiah 29:11, *"For I know the thoughts that I think toward you, saith the Lord, thoughts of peace, and not of evil, to give you an expected end."*

Another revelation I found out about myself is that I was fearful about everything. Scared to go, scared to stay, scared to trust, and scared not to trust. Scared of what people thought about me and felt the need to over explain. What I realized is that people didn't care. My thoughts of my insignificance were brought on by fear and my past. It was not about me, but through my mess, God would be glorified. My life is a gift and was meant to bring honor and glory to God and not a continual pity party.

There have been several gems of knowledge that helped me get to this revelation knowledge. The greatest word that encouraged my heart the most was from Pastor John Gray when he stated, *"They didn't know what you carried, and they treated you like you were common. God wanted them to treat you that way because He wanted you to see who they were."* Powerful words that I keep before me especially when I see the ugliness of people trying to come against me.

Embrace your uniqueness and be the best you, you can be. No one can out do you being you. I had to stop comparing myself to others, walk in my Divine purpose and be who God ordained me to be. I love me. Imperfections and all, because I am fearfully and wonderfully made. Trust the process and know this,

"Being confident of this very thing, that he which hath begun a good work in you will perform it until the day of Jesus Christ."(Philippians 1:6).

Once I forgave myself and realized all I have been through was to shape me into the woman I was meant to be. The renewal was easier. I have referenced several words from the dictionary only to bring clarity to what I am saying. The definition of renew(al) according to *Merriam-Webster* is: to make like new; restore to freshness, vigor, or perfection. I am not perfect, but I strive to be a better me daily. There was purpose in my pain and I pray that everyone who reads this book will be blessed and know that with the help of God you can make it through any of life's challenges.

I have come through some hard lessons, but the good news is I came through. I am still standing and stronger because of it. This is not only my testimony, but so many others who have overcome a few of life's challenges. By sharing my story I am letting you know if I can make it, then you can also.

"Humble yourselves therefore under the mighty hand of God, that he may exalt you in due time: Casting all your care upon him; for he careth for you."

—1 Peter 5:6-7

CHAPTER SIX

Walking in Freedom

My definition of freedom is: being my authentic self; no apologies and loving the skin I'm in.Nolonger seeking anyone's approval, but trusting God and knowing as long as my actions please Him, then I am good. I am more determined than ever to walk this thing out called life; to accomplish all God has planned for me.

There was a prayer I kept on my desk at work and I would like to share, the author is unknown.

A Prayer to Let Go

Dear Lord,

This situation is toxic to my soul, and I need your help, strength, and support. Please help me to know the right steps to take next. Please help me to release fears and insecurity about making this change and trust in your divine wisdom and care.

"Humble yourselves therefore under the mightyhand of God, that he may exalt you in due time. Casting all your care upon him, for he careth for you."(1 Peter 5:6)

This chapter in life and in this book is still being developed as I am walking this out. Everything I have gone through is to bring me to now. The woman I am destined to be.

I am learning daily how to trust God in this process. Trusting God does not mean we do nothing, but we seek to find the path we were created to make. This means find what makes you happy or what do you think about every day that you see yourself doing. Whether it is going back to school, finishing school, or pursuing a craft. Do it!

God has given us everything we need pertaining to life and godliness. Meaning everything we need to do or accomplish is already inside of us and it's up to us to push through to get to it. I love people and enjoy talking to people. My daughter and I always say we never meet a stranger because people will come up to us and start telling us personal things about themselves. It seems to always happen in the grocery store.

She also would tell me I should have been a social worker because no matter what job I had I always became the mom of the department. A welcoming presence is what I strive to display. The smile people use to hide their pain is sometimes hard to recognize but if you connect with someone and truly become a friend it can be easier. The Golden Rule maybe old fashioned to many, but it's what I live by, treat others the way you want to be treated.

The essence of this book is to live the life you have been dealt. No matter how your life started, you

have the ability to change and re-shape your future. If you don't like where your life is taking you, change it.

Strive to be kind, remember life is not about you, but who you affect while you are here. My desire is to please God and that my life bring Him glory because for so long it did not, and He loved me anyway.

While you have read my story, I hope you reflect on your own story. We all face challenges every day and we an either succumb to our test or we overcome our test. If you fail a test like I have so many times get back up and keep moving forward. Don't stay there. Be encouraged and remember:

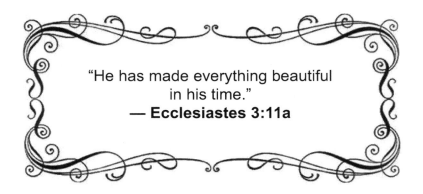

"He has made everything beautiful in his time."
— **Ecclesiastes 3:11a**

CHAPTER SEVEN

Wrap Up

This journey and process of my life has allowed me to learn some valuable lessons. I have adapted to living my life according to my own wisdom principles. My first acknowledgement is that I am not in control of all my situations, but I am in control of how I respond to them. I am no longer living in a place of self-pity or low self-esteem. I know my worth and will no longer settle. It has taken me years to get to this place and I will not relinquish this feeling of freedom. I love me.

Secondly, I won't be afraid to open my heart to love because now it is not coming from a place of desperation or me trying to fix someone because I see their potential. It is not my job to fix anyone outside of myself. I know who I am now.

My third principle and the one I live by the most is this, "I don't have to answer for how you treat me, but I do have to answer for how I treat you." When I say answer for, I am referring to answering to God for my treatment of others. This is a faith walk for me and for so long my life did not honor God. I understand I am not perfect, but we can strive daily to do our best and be our best and pray that along the way our lives affect someone in a positive way.

Everyone was put here to do something. Seek to find your purpose and who you were called to be. We are life changers and the first change must begin with us.

You can do this.

Final Thoughts

What do I expect my life to look like now? I expect my life to look like whatever I choose. No longer held back by fears but ready to pursue every dream that is inside of me. Those dreams that have been dormant are about to be birthed. I am excited about what God is doing in me and through me. I know He is not done with me.

Great things, great things, that is what I am expecting. In other words, I'm living my best life. I challenge you to do the same. Until the next time.

About the Author

Doreen Grady has always had a love for people. She can often be found sharing a smile, and a word of encouragement to thos in need. Her desire is to see people live up to their fullest potential. It has taken her some time to get this revelation in her life and the endurance of many personal trials and tribulations. If she can help anyone fulfill their destiny by sharing her story, she believes we all win. Her new life motto is,"*Know* your worth, believe in yourself, and walk in yourpurpose."

Made in the USA
Middletown, DE
06 September 2024

60512318R00033